The Dark Side of the Millennium

The Problem of Evil in Revelation 20:1–10

Arthur H. Lewis

BAKER BOOK HOUSE
Grand Rapids, Michigan 49506

Preface

An earlier and more concise edition of this study was presented at the 1977 annual meeting of the Evangelical Theological Society, held on the campus of Simpson College in San Francisco. The title then was: "The Problem of Evil in the Millennium." Sufficient interest was generated at that time to encourage me to attempt this more general discussion for lay readers as well as Bible students and teachers.

For whatever reasons, premillennial commentaries on Revelation and books about Bible prophecy have paid meager attention to the fact that Revelation 20 presents the millennial society as a mixture of saints and sinners. The Gog and Magog nations revolt against the King at the end of the thousand years, but they exist as groups of wicked people throughout the entire course of the age. This aspect immediately raises a doubt about the correlation of the millennium with the other kingdom passages in the Bible, which invariably speak of its glory and perfection. So serious is this darker side of the picture that it may prove to be the "Achilles heel" of the entire millennarian system of interpretation.

I believe, therefore, that a fresh study of the wicked nations in Revelation 20 is long overdue. It is time for all students of biblical eschatology to reconsider the full implications of a continuing mixture of the good and the bad after the Messiah's return.

The title of this discussion, *The Dark Side of the Millennium,* also requires an explanation on my part. In most types of literature today, *millennium* almost invariably refers to some future paradise or utopia. Unfortunately this is not the biblical meaning of the term. When properly defined by the language of the only passage in which it occurs in the Bible, the millennium is very different from a state of perfection. For the writer of Revelation the coming paradise is to be found in chapters 21 and 22, not in chapter 20. However, since the future messianic kingdom is indeed a true paradise, it follows that the "millennium is not the age to come."

I am aware that the mere suggestion of this idea will create shock waves for many Christians today. My intention is not to deny the reality of the millennium, but to explode the popular notions that have arisen concerning its place in the stream of events. The point of view herein defended is not *amillennial,* if that label means a negation of a real millennial age. Rather, it should be called *historical millennialism,* since it will assert the present reality of all aspects of the "thousand years" as described in Revelation 20:1–10.

I find it necessary to assume a polemic attitude at the outset of this study in order to show the importance of the subject and the failure of current millennial publications to do it justice. Then I will proceed with a comparative analysis of the kingdom texts throughout the Scriptures by placing them side by side with the millennial passage in Revelation. Finally, I will interpret the main features of Revelation 20:1–10, in the light of their immediate context.

It is my hope that we may embark together on a fresh review of all the important data in the Bible related to this theme, and that my readers will withhold their conclusions until all of the evidence has been examined and the arguments are complete.

Arthur H. Lewis

Contents

Introduction

Will children be born with sinful natures during the age to come, and will great numbers of these children literally go to the devil? Yes, reply many of our most prominent evangelical Bible teachers. One writer has playfully labeled these children "the kingdom kids"—the benighted sons of the saints who will populate the messianic age, but who will be doomed (many of them, at least) to unbelief and eternal destruction.

By assuming that the thousand-year period of Revelation 20 is identical with the oft-mentioned future kingdom of Christ, these teachers are forced to accept the fact that sin and death will play an integral part in the coming age. John Walvoord leaves no doubt about his views on this subject: "The children born to the tribulation saints will far outnumber their parents; they too will be subject to Christ's reign and, if openly rebellious, they will be put to death. It seems obvious that some of these will not be born again, and of these the company of those who rebel against Christ will be formed."[1]

---

1. John F. Walvoord, *The Millennial Kingdom* (Grand Rapids: Dunham, 1959), pp. 316-317.

9

According to J. D. Pentecost, "The progeny born during the millennial age will be born with the same fallen nature with which their parents were born."[2] In complete agreement is Hal Lindsey, who observes that "at the end of the thousand years the unbelieving children rebel, Christ judges them, then He completely changes the old heaven and earth and creates a new one."[3]

It is clear, then, that a popular view exists which asserts that the Messiah, after He returns to earth and establishes His glorious kingdom, will allow unbelievers and wicked nations to develop under His domain. He will also permit many of the sons born in His kingdom to be deceived by Satan and attempt to destroy the saints at the close of the thousand years.

It will be demonstrated later that this dark scene, the revolt of the wicked nations, is based upon the language of Revelation 20 and belongs to any view that takes the millennium literally. But can it be harmonized with the rest of the scriptural prophecies about the messianic kingdom and the age to come?

"The whole problem is admittedly difficult," said Lewis Sperry Chafer some years ago. "It is difficult to understand how such an enterprise will be possible with Christ on the throne."[4] Most students of the Bible will agree wholeheartedly with Chafer's candid opinion, especially after they have examined for themselves the full context of the revolt by the Gog and Magog nations at the close of the millennium.

It is important, therefore, to understand what the millennium is, according to the one passage in the Bible that defines it. Vague conceptions about a "perfect age," or an "ideal

2. J. D. Pentecost, *Things to Come* (Grand Rapids: Dunham, 1958), p. 549.

3. Hal Lindsey, *The Late Great Planet Earth* (Grand Rapids: Zondervan, 1970), p. 178.

4. Lewis S. Chafer, *Systematic Theology*, 8 vols., (Dallas: Dallas Seminary Press, 1947), vol. 5, p. 361.

earthly kingdom," derive invariably from other passages incorrectly linked to Revelation 20. But it is unfair to pull the term *millennium* out of its natural context in order to solve a problem elsewhere. It can only be defined by the language of the first ten verses of Revelation 20, which read as follows:

> Then I saw an angel coming down from heaven, holding in his hand the key of the bottomless pit and a great chain. And he seized the dragon, that ancient serpent, who is the Devil and Satan, and bound him for a thousand years, and threw him into the pit, and shut it and sealed it over him, that he should deceive the nations no more, till the thousand years were ended. After that he must be loosed for a little while.
>
> Then I saw thrones, and seated on them were those to whom judgment was committed. Also I saw the souls of those who had been beheaded for their testimony to Jesus and for the word of God, and who had not worshiped the beast or its image and had not received its mark on their foreheads or their hands. They came to life, and reigned with Christ a thousand years. The rest of the dead did not come to life until the thousand years were ended. This is the first resurrection. Blessed and holy is he who shares in the first resurrection! Over such the second death has no power, but they shall be priests of God and of Christ, and they shall reign with him a thousand years.
>
> And when the thousand years are ended, Satan will be loosed from his prison and will come out to deceive the nations which are at the four corners of the earth, that is, Gog and Magog, to gather them for battle; their number is like the sand of the sea. And they marched up over the broad earth and surrounded the camp of the saints and the beloved city; but fire came down from heaven and consumed them, and the devil who had deceived them was thrown into the lake of fire and sulphur where the beast and the false prophet were, and they will be tormented day and night for ever and ever.

From this short passage we learn that the nations once deceived by Satan are deceived no more for a thousand years; meanwhile, the martyred and faithful saints are seen as "souls alive and reigning with Christ" for a thousand years. Finally, the nations are again deceived by Satan and march on the saints and the beloved city to destroy the King and His people, only at the last moment to be devoured by fire. This is the millennium in its biblical context and definition.

The aim of this study will be to show that evil is indeed an integral part of the thousand-year period described in Revelation 20; it will, however, also show that this evil is sufficient reason to deny the identification of the millennium with the glorious future kingdom of Christ.

Chapter 1 will argue from the natural meaning of the text—that the wicked not only will participate in the millennium but will actually become far more numerous than the saints themselves! The two most common explanations given by millennarians for this disturbing fact will be critically examined in the second chapter.

Chapters 3 and 4 will take a penetrating look at the major kingdom passages in the Old and New Testaments, in search for some correlation with the millennium as defined in Revelation 20.

Finally, in chapter 5 we will reappraise the significance of the millennium within its immediate context in the Book of Revelation. We will attempt to place it in the sequence of eschatological events. The answer will not grow out of a non-literal hermeneutic or any attempt to "spiritualize" the language of the passage. The reader will have to judge for himself, in light of the exegetical observations and comparative studies presented throughout this discussion, whether or not the basic thesis is valid.

How Evil
Is
the Millennium?

A standard practice of the premillennialists is to portray the coming messianic age as a blend of the old with the new. It is not quite the "new earth" of Revelation 21 and 22, nor is it our present state of affairs, but rather something in between. Thus it is reasoned that since the millennium is the age to come, it must be a mingling of good and bad, saints and sinners, paradise and curse.

Such a view is further necessitated by the urge to find a period when all of the political and material promises to Abraham and David may become literally fulfilled (assuming that no past situation of Israel adequately met those covenantal promises).[1] The land, the throne, the temple, and the twelve tribes must all be restored to the earth in a political context for the Old Testament prophecies to come true; and the Messiah, David's eternal son, will bring this about during the thousand years of Revelation 20. Just as the wicked nations were out

---

1. Rene Pache, *The Return of Jesus Christ* (Chicago: Moody Press, 1955), p. 369.

there surrounding David's realm, so must they be present in the realm of the greater David, the difference being that the Messiah will exercise global power and authority over all peoples and nations.

Without question, the facts in the text of Revelation 20 support at least one part of this viewpoint: iniquitous peoples are indeed active at the close of, and evidently present throughout, the thousand years. No label better describes them than the one the apostle John borrowed from Ezekiel: "Gog and Magog." The authors of the early apocalyptic books of Judaism also utilized this label for the far-flung pagan hordes that existed on the fringes of the known world. These nations always posed a threat to the land and the security of Israel.[2]

This point requires no stress, however, since interpreters from all sides generally agree on the fact of the millennial evil. If anything, the amillennialists tend to place more emphasis on it than the premillennialists; but for them, of course, the mixture of good and bad belongs to this present age. Many "amills" are futurists in the sense that they take the final scene of Revelation 19 with its warfare between the Antichrist and the Messiah to be the same event as the Gog and Magog revolt in chapter 20.

The magnitude of this evil is a matter of dispute among premillennarians. Some try to belittle its importance, while others call the millennial unbelief and revolt against Christ the primary feature of man's last dispensation, proving his failure to follow Christ even with Satan bound! John Walvoord attempts to diminish the problem with these words: "Though it

---

2. Compare the *Sibylline Oracles* (3:512), where the nations led by Gog and Magog are at war with the Messiah. Josephus linked them with the Sythians (*Ant.* 1:6.1; and *Jub.* 8:25). In the Talmud, *Aggadah*, Gog and Magog are usually identified with the nations of Psalm 2 which set themselves against the Lord's Anointed (cf. Ber. 7b, 10a, 13b; Shab. 118a; Pes. 118a; Meg. 11a; and San. 94a, 97b).

is impossible to prove that the majority of the earth's population are saved in the latter days of the millennium, it is safe to assume that a large percentage in any case will really know the Lord."[3] Leon Wood goes even further: "Surely they (the unsaved) will constitute a small minority."[4]

On the other hand, authors such as Charles Ryrie feel that "the saints will appear to be outnumbered,"[5] and Rene Pache admits that "this is the most disconcerting fact of all! After what the prophets have told us about the conversion of the nations, it seems difficult to believe that these rebels represent the majority of men."[6]

What is God's purpose in this final dispensation? The answer, according to James M. Boice, is the need to show how wicked the human race really is. He writes, "This rebellion is the great purpose of the millennium."[7] Boice's conclusion reflects that of his predecessor, Donald G. Barnhouse. In a series of debates on the millennial question held at Gordon Divinity School shortly before his death, Dr. Barnhouse asserted that "the millennial age will be the most iniquitous age of all!" However, he went on to explain, this iniquity will be held in check by Christ and His angels, not permitting any public acts of violence. At the same time the unconverted will continually "seethe within" against the righteous rule of Christ and refuse to believe Him in their hearts.[8] This fits with Walvoord's statement that "Only the *openly* rebellious will be

---

3. John F. Walvoord, *The Millennial Kingdom* (Grand Rapids: Dunham, 1959), p. 317.

4. Leon J. Wood, *The Bible and Future Events* (Grand Rapids: Zondervan, 1973), p. 178.

5. C. C. Ryrie, *The Living End* (Old Tappan, New Jersey: Fleming H. Revell, 1973), p. 126.

6. Rene Pache, *The Return*, p. 432.

7. James M. Boice, *The Last and Future World* (Grand Rapids: Zondervan, 1974), p. 30.

8. Taken from personal notes at Gordon Divinity School during a series of debates on the millennium between Donald Barnhouse and Albertus Pieters in 1956.

put to death."[9] Ryrie says that "some will even despise the King and loathe those who share in His government."[10] But the most curious explanation of all comes from John Phillip's book, *Exploring Revelation:* "As children of believing parents today become gospel-hardened, so during the millennium many will become *glory hardened* [italics mine]; they will render only feigned obedience"[11]

Taking stock of these various opinions, they add up to a strange breed of citizens of the kingdom who pay only lip service to the King while hating him in their hearts. Nothing could be further from the true nature of righteousness as taught by Jesus in His Sermon on the Mount, which, ironically, is usually acclaimed by these very same authors to be the future constitution for the coming age.

Another way to emphasize the gravity of the millennial problem of evil is to show that there will be in that day lost souls who will need the gospel preached to them, just as they do today. "Salvation will be based on the value of the death of Christ and will be appropriated by faith in the millennium," declares J. D. Pentecost.[12] The saints will need to launch in that day "a special millennial missionary effort," according to J. Barton Payne in his massive *Encyclopedia of Biblical Prophecy.*[13] Evidently Payne believes that the task of "preaching the gospel of the kingdom in the whole world as a testimony to all nations" (Matt. 24:14) will not be completed by the end of this age or before the return of Christ. Such a

---

9. J. Walvoord, *Millennial Kingdom,* p. 302.

10. C. C. Ryrie, *Living End,* p. 124.

11. John Phillips, *Exploring Revelation* (Chicago: Moody Press, 1974), p. 282. The analogy has little force since in the presence of the exalted Savior "every knee shall bow" and "every tongue shall confess that Jesus Christ is the Lord" (Phil. 2:10, 11, *Phillips*).

12. J. D. Pentecost, *Things to Come* (Grand Rapids: Dunham, 1958), p. 483.

13. J. Barton Payne, *Encyclopedia of Biblical Prophecy* (New York: Harper and Row, 1973), p. 319.

theory is patently contrary to the admonitions of Christ for all
men to heed and believe now, before the judgment, when it
will be too late (Matt. 13:37–39; 22:8–14; John 12:48). This
view also denies the Lord's clearly stated intention that the
age to come will be for the rewarding of the saints, not for an
extension of evangelism to the lost (Matt. 25:31ff.).

But let us assume for the moment that Payne is correct on
this point, and that lost souls will indeed have still another day
to hear the gospel and be saved. What would it be like to
stand as a sinner in the physical presence of the sovereign,
glorified Son of God, surrounded by the obvious and undeniable evidence of His saving power and victory over Satan, and
then to be asked to accept or reject Him? Would not all
preaching be superfluous under those conditions? It would
not be just another case for a "doubting Thomas," since the
Messiah will be not only resurrected but glorified in His deity
and power, along with the surrounding saints and angels.
Only the reprobate would reject the Lord of glory under those
terms!

What normally would be a dilemma, however, turns out to
be no problem at all for Stanley Ellison, who can talk on the
one hand about the beauties and perfections of the Messiah's
reign on earth, while on the other hand imagine men "sinning
without the Devil's help!" He goes on to say that at the final
act Satan will actually serve the purpose of God by "polarizing
the wicked," and also by "drawing off the dross from God's
kingdom."[14]

For those who are of this persuasion, what unspeakable
pathos will accompany the saints in the age to come! They will
be helpless spectators of these rebel sons of the kingdom, who
must persist in their unconverted state to the very end. What
else can this mean but that righteousness will *not* cover the

---

14. Stanley A. Ellisen, *Biography of a Great Planet* (Wheaton: Tyndale
House, 1975), p. 214.

earth; neither will the love of Christ prevail in all hearts. His reign will be universal only in a superficial sense. This concept of the kingdom can be found nowhere in the Bible. A statement by W. K. Harrison shows the incongruity of this point of view: "The millennial kingdom is the final proof that the natural human heart is incurably wicked, and that apart from the new birth a man cannot see the kingdom of God."[15] But since our Lord in his conversation with Nicodemus (John 3:1-15) was referring to a future reward for believers and born-again souls today, how can he apply this verse to the sinners who will make up an integral part of that kingdom? It is absurd to warn the wicked that they will "not see the kingdom," when they are basking in its benefits!

With all of this concern by the premillennarians to get the "kingdom kids" converted, it is odd that the term *grace* is never encountered in any of their descriptions of the future kingdom of Christ. Certainly it must be obvious to them that apart from the grace and mercy of God no sinner will ever be saved! Their silence about grace and its necessity after the Lord's return is probably due to the silence of the Scriptures on the subject. Today, "is the day of salvation," said Paul (II Cor. 6:2). Grace has been essential for the forgiveness of sinners from the moment of Adam's fall, and will be essential up to the very last day when heaven's offer of deliverance is forever closed (cf. II Peter 3:8-13).

The facts pointing to the enormous size of the Gog and Magog nations have been clearly indicated in the text. Their number "is like the sand of the sea" (Rev. 20:8). They march "over the broad earth"; that is, over the entire breadth of it (20:9). They completely surround the saints contained in their "beloved city" (20:9), which premillennialists insist means the literal and local site of Jerusalem. Whether the language is

---

15. W. K. Harrison, *Hope Triumphant* (Chicago: Moody Press, 1966), pp. 108-109.

taken literally or symbolically, the disproportion of the evil to the good is patent in the text. Once again, as has happened so often throughout the history of the people of God, the wicked outnumber the righteous. This fact, of course, would not be surprising within the context of our present world, but when it is cast into the glorious and victorious reign of the Messiah it is nothing short of unbelievable!

Summary

This chapter has demonstrated that the problem of evil in the millennium will not go away by simply ignoring it. Alongside the earthly saints reside the rebellious ones, men not free to commit public transgressions but able to despise the Lord in their hearts while standing in His very presence. This will happen, premillennarians would have us believe, in the Messiah's future kingdom on earth.

In sharp contrast with the difficulties encountered by the popular view is the ease with which *historical millennialism* interprets these same passages. When the "thousand years" is understood to be coterminous with this day and age, the pieces all fall in place. Unbelief, sin, war, and death belong to the present and will intensify at the time of the "great tribulation" just before the return of Christ. Therefore, the dark side of the millennium strongly suggests that it is not future but actual.

Chapter Two

How Will
the Wicked
Get In?

All millennarians agree that evil men and nations will populate the messianic kingdom, but there is a division of the house as to the way they will get into the millennium. Pretribulationists have one explanation for the origin of the wicked, and posttribulationists have another.

The pretribulationists would appear to have a special advantage in this regard since their view allows for seven extra years to prepare for the millennium which follows. Resurrected saints, of course, will never again bear sons and daughters (Matt. 22:30), but if souls are won to Christ after the rapture and resurrection of the dead, these "saints" of the tribulation will still be in their natural bodies and will be able to give birth to children with sinful and Adamic natures, just as they do today. From these offspring of the surviving tribulation saints will come the wicked of the following age.

For Hal Lindsey this idea is so important that he actually calls it "the chief reason" in favor of a pretribulation rapture! He argues that "if the rapture took place at the same time as the second coming, there would be no mortals left who would be believers: therefore, there would be no one to go into the kingdom and repopulate the earth."[1] A similar conclusion comes from *The Bible and Future Events* by Leon Wood: "At the beginning no unsaved persons will exist, but as children are born, some will show this rebellion and how desperately wicked the heart of man is by nature."[2] Neither Lindsey nor Wood offers any scriptural evidence in support of this view, which is inferential at best. Logic is never a substitute for exegesis, particularly when other passages raise serious doubts concerning the survival of any wicked persons after the Messiah's return for the express purpose of judging "the quick and the dead" (Acts 10:42, KJV).

The pretribulationists, therefore, have a logical explanation for the evil in the millennium, which grows out of their departmentalizing of the Lord's return into two phases. Their seven-year extension of the age enables some to come to the Lord but miss the resurrection. To this they would add their theory that the Davidic kingdom to come will have an environment similar to the one found in the Old Testament when the Lord's covenant promises to Israel were pronounced. It is taken for granted that every dispensation must end in disaster and judgment—even the one Christ will govern!

Posttribulational millennarians do not have this seeming advantage. Their perspective places the rapture and resurrection at "the last day," and at the close of the tribulation. Thus, no saints will survive and enter the following age in their earthly bodies with the capacity to bear children. All will have been either resurrected and glorified and will "be like the angels," or else condemned and sent into hell. Or will they? Somehow, the wicked nations reemerge in that future kingdom of the Messiah. George Ladd refuses to speculate on

---

1. Hal Lindsey, *The Late Great Planet Earth* (Grand Rapids: Zondervan, 1970), p. 143.

2. Leon J. Wood, *The Bible and Future Events* (Grand Rapids: Zondervan, 1973), p. 178.

their origin, however. He simply asserts their presence: "Even in such a (righteous) age, the hearts of men remain rebellious and respond to the Devil when he is released."[3] His interpretation suggests a certain overlapping of the present with the future phases of the kingdom. Like the Jewish *chiliasts*, Ladd believes in an earthly reign of Christ which will be in many ways no different from this present age.

Robert Gundry is more specific in his explanation. In his recently published book, *The Church and the Tribulation*, he claims "that it can be demonstrated that some of the wicked will survive the tribulation and Parousia, and that those who do will enter the millennium."[4] However, Gundry's "demonstration" turns out to be only one conditional phrase in one Old Testament text which reads: "And if any of the families of the earth do not go up to Jerusalem to worship the King, the Lord of hosts, there will be no rain upon them" (Zech. 14:17). From this passage he concludes that since some will refuse to worship the king, they will constitute a wicked element in the Messiah's realm. But the text of Zechariah does not say for a fact that the "refusers" will be there; this is a conditional or hypothetical clause which at best suggests that there might be such families. The meaning is dubious and may be taken either way. Parallel passages will be surveyed in the following chapter which show that only the converted nations will be allowed a part in the Messiah's reign of peace on earth.

Both Gundry and Ladd must face the explicit declarations in the New Testament to the effect that *all* of the wicked will perish at or before the Lord's return. Nothing remotely suggests that some of the evildoers of this age will manage to slip by the final judgments and reappear within the realm of the King and His future glory. The evidence for this follows.

---

3. George Ladd, *The Last Things* (Grand Rapids: W. B. Eerdmans, 1978), p. 110.

4. Robert H. Gundry, *The Church and the Tribulation* (Grand Rapids: Zondervan, 1973), p. 166.

Jesus used categorical terms in Matthew 13 about the fate of the "weeds" which are destined to be "gathered out of His kingdom . . . and cast into the furnace of fire" (Matt. 13:41, 42). His discourses match the teachings of His parables, for the flood "came and took them all away. That is how it will be at the coming of the Son of Man" (Matt. 24:39). Again, in Matthew 25 He taught that, "when the son of Man comes in his glory, . . . he will sit on his throne in heavenly glory and all the nations will be gathered before him. . . . Then he will say to those on his left, Depart from me, you who are cursed, into the eternal fire prepared for the devil and his angels."

It is not surprising that Paul taught the same thing as Jesus on the subject of the doom of all the wicked at the close of this age. To the Thessalonians he wrote:

> . . . those who do not know God and who do not obey the Gospel of our Lord Jesus Christ . . . will be punished with everlasting destruction and shut out from the presence of the Lord and from the majesty of his power on the day he comes to be . . . marveled at among all those who have believed
> (II Thess. 1:8–10, NIV).

If there are to be any exceptions to this declaration by Paul, if some of the wicked will in fact escape the destruction of that hour of judgment, as Gundry and the posttribulationists seem to believe, then Paul has seriously confused the picture. On the other hand, if Paul has fully and accurately explained the fate of the wicked, then this passage leaves no place for the posttribulationists' view.

Peter's teaching on the events connected with the return of the Lord closely resembles Paul's. He warned all scoffers that the longsuffering of Christ would not continue forever; the open door for repentant sinners would close abruptly at His coming.

> The Lord is not slow about his promise as some count slowness, but is forbearing toward you, not wishing that any should

perish, but that all should reach repentance. But the day of the
Lord will come like a thief, and then the heavens will pass
away with a loud noise, and the elements will be dissolved
with fire, and the earth and the works that are upon it will be
burned up (II Peter 3:9, 10).

This total destruction foreseen by Peter must signal the death
of all evil men as well.

Finally we come to the battle scene in Revelation 19 where
John delineates the doom of all who will follow the Beast.
There will be no place to escape; "all men, both free and
slave, both small and great" will die and become carrion for
the birds to eat. "And the rest were slain by the sword of him
who sits upon the horse" (Rev. 19:21).

In the light of these New Testament passages and their
concurrence on this theme, it appears undeniable that there is
no biblical support for the idea that evil men or wicked nations will manage to slip by the judgments set for the end of
this age. John Walvoord correctly summarized the scriptural
view by saying, "All the wicked will be put to death after the
second coming of Christ."[5]

Looking back over this chapter we find that neither the
pretribulationists nor the posttribulationists have produced an
adequate exegetical foundation for their common assertion
that evil nations will reappear during the Messiah's future
reign.

---

5. John F. Walvoord, *The Millennial Kingdom* (Grand Rapids: Dunham,
1959), p. 302.

Chapter Three

Is There
an Old Testament
Millennium?

How is the age to come viewed from the perspective of the Old Testament? Does it bear any resemblance to the state of affairs described in Revelation 20:1–10? If the answer, after careful investigation and comparison, is negative, then one of the major tenets of the millennarian system of interpretation will certainly be in doubt, namely, the belief that the Hebrew prophets foresaw the thousand-year reign of Christ.

The issue of hermeneutical principles is not critical to this investigation, since it can be shown that even when the Old Testament kingdom passages are taken in their most obvious and literal sense, there still will exist a wide gap between them and the millennial scene in Revelation 20. It is understandable that the student of biblical prophecy would try to find some historical situation to correspond to each and every prediction concerning the future of Israel and the Messiah. Yet no amount of anxiety in trying to make the "Bible come true" will justify a wrong usage of the kingdom passages. Certain aspects of the messianic vision came into reality with the return of the exiles to Jerusalem in 536 B.C. under the decree of Cyrus. Others waited for the birth of the "shoot from the stump of Jesse" (Isa. 11:1) and the establishment of the spiritual kingdom by Christ. Still others are waiting for the end of this age and the inauguration of the age to come (see chart, p. 29). The issue is not one of hermeneutics but of identification. Where in this eschatological spectrum does the scene from Revelation 20:1–10 fit in? (See chart 1.)

The predictions in the Old Testament concerning the wars to be fought by the Messiah against the nations offer a good starting point for this investigation. When and under what conditions will these battles take place?

First, we must eliminate the historical conflicts which the prophets foresaw in the immediate future. Amos predicted the siege of Samaria by the Assyrians; Joel saw an army of "grasshoppers," which some relate to the events of the ninth century while others take it to refer to the devastation of Jerusalem by the Babylonians. Second, we need to find some clear indication in the text that the wars are for judgment and for determining the final destination of the nations involved; there must be evidence, therefore, that they rightfully belong to the *eschaton*. Finally, we will have to ask whether the wars of the nations against the Messiah can be placed before, during, or after the "day of the Lord," since only those wars scheduled to occur after His return could have any possible relationship to the state of affairs within His kingdom.

The Messianic Psalms

Psalm 2 takes a heavenly viewpoint in which the Lord looks down and laughs at the puny efforts of the nations to oppose his Anointed. The impending battle never transpires, as the Lord speaks out in His wrath, demanding of the nations that all powers be surrendered to the authority of His Son; the nations are then to become His possession and heritage. First,

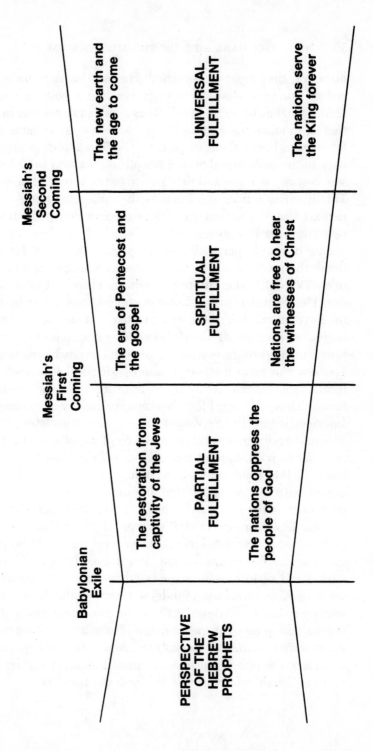

THE FULFILLMENT OF OLD TESTAMENT PROPHECY

PERSPECTIVE OF THE HEBREW PROPHETS

Babylonian Exile

The restoration from captivity of the Jews

PARTIAL FULFILLMENT

The nations oppress the people of God

Messiah's First Coming

The era of Pentecost and the gospel

SPIRITUAL FULFILLMENT

Nations are free to hear the witnesses of Christ

Messiah's Second Coming

The new earth and the age to come

UNIVERSAL FULFILLMENT

The nations serve the King forever

however, they must be punished. He will "break them with a
rod of iron, and dash them in pieces like a potter's vessel"
(2:9). It makes no sense to take these actions in reverse order;
that is, to make the nations His possession and heritage, then
later on to break them in pieces. The "breaking" is preliminary to the possessing! So the people are warned to "Kiss the
son, lest he be angry and they perish in the way" (2:12a, KJV).
Totally missing from the Psalm is the millennial scene of evil
nations thriving within the King's domain and permitted to
revolt against His power.

One phrase in particular needs special attention: "He shall
break them with a rod of iron," *break* coming from the verb
ra'a', רעע (2:9). The Hebrew words are clear and unambigu-
ous. However, the same phrase is quoted three times by John
in Revelation, but with *rule* instead of *break* (*rule*, or
shepherd, is *ra'ah*, רעה in Hebrew). The reason for this alteration is obvious to those who can read the original language. In
Hebrew the term for *rule* is almost identical in sound, different only by one letter in spelling, to the term meaning
break. Thus, the word for *shepherd*, or *rule*, was mistakenly
interjected into the Septuagint (the Greek translation of the
Hebrew Scriptures), and from the Septuagint it was carried
into the New Testament text. Some will discount the importance of this change by noting that the *rod* is usually associated with the work of the shepherd, sometimes for the
protection of the sheep and other times for their punishment.

John, however, does not misrepresent the original meaning
of the Psalm, even though he employed the other word as
given in his Greek translation. For John, the act of "ruling
with a rod of iron" was a single climactic event, associated
with the King's final war of judgment against the Beast and all
who carry his mark (Rev. 19:15). In an earlier reference (2:27)
the apostle quotes the entire text of Psalm 2:9, making *ruling*
parallel with *shattering* the nations. Again, the concept is best
considered as one act or event of punishment, not a description of a harsh rule with the rod for a thousand years.

The error is not John's for putting *rule* in the New Testament quotation, but the error of many interpreters who have wrongly imagined what *rule* means. If it means that Christ will be ruling throughout the millennium with a "rod of iron" in His hand, then logically there will have to be wicked people who need such firm treatment. But this also suggests that these enemies of the Messiah will challenge His authority with repeated deeds of violence and rebellion. Neither the language of Psalm 2 nor the use of it by John in the Book of Revelation warrants such a conclusion.

A study of Psalm 110 will yield the same essential facts which were given in the Psalm 2 concerning the time of the final messianic wars. Victory again is a foregone conclusion, for the King will sit on His throne until all of His enemies become His "footstool." When the day for battle approaches, however, He is seen leading forth His people as a great army "upon the holy mountains" (110:3). Then, with one swift act of judgment, the one on the throne "will shatter kings on the day of his wrath. He will execute judgment among the nations, filling them with corpses" (110:5b, 6a). This is hardly a peaceful millennial scene! It does fit, however, with the final events associated with the "great and terrible day of the Lord" marked for the close of *this* age.

Some exegetes have tried to identify the psalm with the millennium by making the Lord on His throne a type of reigning Messiah in the age to come. But it just won't work; at least, it will not work for a reign of conflict and warfare sequential to Christ's return in triumph. Both Peter and Paul use this psalm to describe the Lord's present-day task of shattering his enemies. Peter's view on the day of Pentecost is not that of a Christ in glory, waiting to start His reign at some future date, but that of a victorious and ascended Christ whose enemies are even now in the process of being destroyed. For both the psalmist and the apostle, the throne is a heavenly one and the battle a spiritual one, but the age is this present one!

Paul quotes this very same phrase from Psalm 110:1, and with the same interpretation that Peter gave to it. "For he must reign until he has put all enemies under his feet. The last enemy to be destroyed is death" (I Cor. 15:25, 26). For Paul, the Lord's victories were in the present tense, proven by the obvious fact that the time for the "last enemy" to be destroyed coincides with the resurrection day at the close of this age. "Death is swallowed up in victory" (15:54), not after a delay of one thousand years, but coincident with the "last trumpet," when the dead shall be raised imperishable. For the apostle Paul, this moment will take place at the very end of this present age. Only then will the victorious Son present His kingdom to the Father, having destroyed "every rule and every authority and power" (15:24).

If the New Testament explains the Old Testament, and if Peter at Pentecost and Paul in writing to the Corinthians knew what they were talking about, the so called messianic wars against the evil nations and the spiritual powers of Satan are part of this present day and age. The ascension and return to the throne announced Christ's ultimate victory over all His enemies, and the resurrection of the dead will complete His victory.

The Kingdom of the Prophets

Many Bible teachers believe that they can find the same millennium of Revelation 20 in the predictions of the Old Testament prophets. Isaiah 11, for example, is often associated with the millennial kingdom.

But with righteousness he shall judge the poor,
    and decide with equity for the meek of the earth;
and he shall smite the earth with the rod of his mouth,
    and with the breath of his lips he shall slay the wicked (Isa. 11:4).

This is indeed a beautiful promise of justice for the poor, but does it provide us with a typical scene to be repeated throughout the thousand years, or rather, a scene preliminary to the future kingdom? If life in that day will be so insecure that the King must constantly smite down the enemies of the poor, then obviously they will have to live in perpetual danger. The good King will never quite manage to eliminate His problems. But this is absurd and cannot be the intended meaning of Isaiah. Nor does this view fit the rest of the passage in chapter 11, where we find that righteousness will characterize the Lord's future kingdom, not violence! Corresponding to the blessed state of the righteous, all nature will be turned into a paradise like the garden of Eden. "They shall not hurt or destroy in all my holy mountain; for the earth shall be full of the knowledge of the Lord as the waters cover the sea" (Isa. 11:9). Furthermore, a desire to worship will rise up from all corners of the earth as all peoples and nations seek Him and His glory. The smiting of the wicked nations, therefore, is associated with the kingdom, but is not typical of the course of the kingdom; rather, it has to do with the elimination of all injustice at its inception.

How did the New Testament writers understand this passage from Isaiah? Paul quotes from it in his second letter to the Thessalonians, warning them against the "man of lawlessness" who is due to appear at the end of this age. When Christ returns to this earth, He "will slay him with the breath of his mouth and destroy him by his appearing and [parousia] his coming" (II Thess. 2:8). Clearly the apostle Paul applied the text from Isaiah to the event of His coming, and not to the state of affairs during the future kingdom.

John also utilizes the language of Isaiah in connection with the final judgment on the Beast and his evil followers. When all of the armies gather to make war on the Messiah, John sees the hosts of heaven arrayed behind the King on His white horse. "From his mouth issues a sharp sword with which to smite the nations" (Rev. 19:15). The King then makes use of the "rod of iron," and all of the wicked are slain "by the sword of him who sits up on the horse, the sword that issues from his mouth" (19:21). The righteous word of the Lord on that day of war and judgment will put an end to all of the satanic forces of evil. Thus John also assures us that such dark moments of conflict belong to the consummation of this age and will not reoccur in the glorious kingdom that follows.

Prophecies from Zechariah also are associated by the pre-millennials with the course of the age to come. There are wars in Zechariah 12 and 14 which are waged against the Holy City by evil nations which appear to be very similar to those in Ezekiel 38 and 39. One difference, however, is that in the attacks visualized by Zechariah, Jerusalem is actually captured for a while. "Lo, I am about to make Jerusalem a cup of reeling to all the peoples round about" (12:2). Later he says of the city, "the houses plundered and the women ravished; half of the city shall go into exile" (14:2). This devastation is too much, even for the attack foreseen by John in Revelation 20 under Gog and Magog. Jerusalem, of course, was captured and destroyed repeatedly throughout the course of history and could suffer such ruin again in the future. But nothing in Zechariah suggests that a disaster of these proportions, or even the threat of one like this, could ever take place once the Messiah has firmly established His future kingdom of peace. To the contrary, about that day the prophet exclaims, "for there shall be no more curse; Jerusalem shall dwell in security" (Zech. 14:11). In fact, every part and detail of the King's domain will be cleansed and sanctified—even the bells of the horses will read "Holy to the Lord!" (14:20).

The prophet Micah foretold the wonderful day when the messianic kingdom will be founded in Zion. As one might expect, he envisions only perpetual peace and prosperity:

> And they shall beat their swords into plowshares,
>   and their spears into pruning hooks;

> nation shall not lift up sword against nation,
> neither shall they learn war any more (Mic. 4:3).

Micah could have heard these same words from his contemporary, Isaiah, who recorded them also (Isa. 2:4). The endless tranquility of the kingdom is guaranteed by another one of Isaiah's predictions about the Davidic child: "Of the increase of *his* government and peace *there shall be* no end" (Isa. 9:7, KJV).

Jeremiah strongly differs with the premillennial theory that the righteousness of many will be merely superficial, or "feigned," as one author put it. Speaking of a future day when not even the ark of the covenant would be remembered or missed, he said:

> At that time Jerusalem shall be called the throne of the Lord, and all nations shall gather to it, to the presence of the Lord in Jerusalem, and they shall no more stubbornly follow their own evil heart" (Jer. 3:17).

Furthermore, according to Jeremiah, there shall be a new covenant and "they shall all know me, from the least of them to the greatest, . . . for I will forgive their iniquity, and I will remember their sin no more" (31:34b). If there are any who insist that this particular promise is for Israel only and therefore not applicable to the final kingdom of Christ, let them consider again the plain teaching of Christ and Paul about the extent of the new covenant, which will open the door to all men and nations and provide by his blood a redemption for "whosoever will" (Mark 14:24; I Cor. 11:23–26; 12:12, 13; Eph. 2:11–13).

The prophecy about Gog and the nations in the Book of Ezekiel is especially important to this discussion. Since John referred to Gog and Magog as a symbol of the wicked nations, the interpretation of Ezekiel 38 and 39 is crucial to the argument. Most of the peoples mentioned by Ezekiel have now been identified by the students of archaeology. Meshech and

Tubal are linked to old city-states in northern Turkey, ancient Cappadocia. Gomer is tied phonetically to Crimaea, which was a nation first located south of the Black Sea, then to the west of it. Put was in the region of modern Libya, and Cush in Upper Egypt, modern Sudan, or Ethiopia. Russia is never mentioned, the nation farthest to the north being Beth-togarmath. Persia represents the easternmost land; and so from all sides the enemies come under the command of Gog, "chief prince of Meshech and Tubal."[1]

Many invasions of Palestine by distant nations actually took place during the intertestamental period, as Daniel's predictions also indicate, and the literal aspects of the battle, such as the "wooden weapons," which required seven years to burn up, best fit into this early period when attacks were made by the Persians, Sythians, Greeks, and others. But rabbinic as well as Christian scholars have seen Ezekiel's "Gog of Magog" as a symbol of evil forces which will rise up to fight against the Messiah at the end of the age. Jesus also may have referred to this prophecy when He remarked, "Wherever the body is, there the eagles will be gathered together" (Matt. 24:28; cf. Ezek. 39:17). Certainly the writer of Revelation 19:21 had Ezekiel in mind when he spoke of the "birds gorged with their flesh," the carrion left from the battle of the King against the Beast and all who had his mark. Once again the words of both Christ and John tie the Gog invasion to the events of the last tribulation and the second coming. John Walvoord correctly sees this truth: "The Gog and Magog in Ezekiel 38:2 is an event referring to a battle which probably precedes the millennium; it should not be confused with the battle in Revelation 20:8."[2]

---

1. Emil G. Kraeling, *Rand McNally Bible Atlas* (New York: Rand McNally & Company, 1946), p. 48. Kraeling's summary of the Table of Nations in Genesis 10 shows how extensive has been the identification of ancient place names. For greater detail see J. Simons, *The Geographical and Topographical Texts of the Old Testament* (Leiden: E. J. Brill, 1937).

2. John F. Walvoord, *The Millennial Kingdom* (Grand Rapids: Dunham, 1959), p. 302.

One isolated text in the prophets, however, would appear to be contradictory. Isaiah 65:20 is without doubt a passage that concerns the age to come, the messianic kingdom. Yet it says that both sin and death will occur after a "hundred years." The entire verse reads as follows:

> No more shall there be in it (Jerusalem)
> an infant that lives but a few days,
> or an old man who does not fill out his days,
> for the child shall die a hundred years old,
> and the sinner a hundred years old shall
> be accursed.

Taken literally it seems to mean that no baby will die in infancy and that all will live to be one hundred, then die. No sinner will be cursed when he sins, but only after one hundred years. On the other hand, the same paragraph contradicts this by telling of a kingdom where "no more shall be heard in it the sound of weeping" (65:19). The children "shall be the offspring of the blessed of the Lórd" (65:23). The wild beasts "shall not hurt or destroy in all my holy mountain" (65:25). Thus the literal sense is denied by the total context of the passage. How could parents in that day have any joy or hope, knowing that their children will die when they reach the age of one hundred? Such an environment would become a horror instead of a paradise! All attempts at finding a solution to this passage seem to fall short; even the translation of the text of Isaiah 65:20 is problematical.[3] If we may assume, however, that Isaiah often saw the future reign of the Lord in limited and metaphoric terms, the following paraphrase may be close to what he was getting at: "No baby ever again will die in childbirth, and no sinner will ever again be accursed."

---

3. The *New International Version* for Isaiah 65:20 reads:
   "He who dies at a hundred will be thought a mere youth;
   He who fails to reach a hundred will be considered accursed."
The Hebrew for "the one who sins" is taken to mean "the one who misses the mark" of one hundred. The easier reading is found in the RSV: "and the sinner a hundred years old shall be accursed."

Summary

Looking back over the royal psalms and the kingdom passages in the prophetic books, we must conclude that the points in common with Revelation 20:1–10 either do not exist or they pull the situation of the nations back into this present age. The conflicts belong to the final judgments, then everlasting peace and security follow upon the establishing of the King's realm. The knowledge of the Lord and His righteousness will not be "skin-deep," but total and pervasive. The earth is to become a universal paradise. No hint can be found of any distant revolt by enemy nations once the Lord's government on earth has begun.

From the perspective of the Old Testament the Messiah's coming was to be a single event, not two or three. And because they could only see one advent of the Messiah, they saw only one kingdom to follow, the perfect and eternal one. Therefore, it is much easier to harmonize the various Old Testament views of the messianic kingdom with the final state in Revelation 21 and 22 than with the intermediate and imperfect millennial state in Revelation 20.

Chapter Four

Is the New Testament Kingdom the Millennium?

In the opinion of most New Testament scholars the messianic kingdom is both "now and "not yet." Its immediate phase has to do with the rule of Christ in the hearts and lives of His followers. He taught: "If it is by the finger of God that I cast out demons, then the kingdom of God has come upon you" (Luke 11:20). John ended the era of the law and the prophets; . . . "since then the good news of the kingdom of God is preached, and everyone enters it violently" (Luke 16:16). Again in Luke the Lord affirmed the same fact: "The kingdom of God is not coming with signs to be observed . . . for behold, the kingdom of God is in the midst of you" (Luke 17:20, 21). The King himself has come and now stands in the midst of His own. Matthew recorded Jesus to say that "the gospel of the kingdom will be preached throughout the whole world, as a testimony to all nations, and then the end will come" (Matt. 24:14). This work of taking the good news to all nations is the theme of the Book of Acts, in which the kingdom is mentioned as the reign of Christ over his followers (Acts 14:22; 19:8;

39

28:23). And Paul, to add one further bit of evidence, assured the Colossians that "he has delivered us from the dominion of darkness and transferred us to the kingdom of his beloved Son" (Col. 1:13).

But the future phase of the kingdom is equally salient in the New Testament. We are taught by our Lord to pray "Thy kingdom come." In the parables of the kingdom found in Matthew 13, both phases are clearly distinguishable. The kingdom is moving even now in the world, growing and thriving in the midst of thorns and satanic opposition. But in the coming final day of judgment the wicked will be destroyed and the righteous will enter the future kingdom where they "will shine like the sun in the kingdom of their Father" (Matt. 13:43). At the Last Supper Jesus said, "I shall not drink again of the fruit of the vine until that day when I drink it new in the kingdom of God" (Mark 14:25).

It is this future kingdom that must be carefully compared with the millennium in order to ascertain if the two are identical or not. Again it is essential that the meaning of *millennium* be restricted to the language given it in Revelation 20. We may not in all fairness compare the New Testament kingdom passages to those already discussed in the Old Testament, as if they too were the millennium. Yet one part of the millennial scene does bear some similarities with the kingdom in the Gospels: the part concerning "saints beheaded and reigning with Christ for a thousand years." This could be paired with the predictions of Jesus about those faithful disciples who had given up everything to follow Him. "Truly, I say to you, in the new world, when the Son of man shall sit on his glorious throne, you who have followed me will also sit on twelve thrones, judging the twelve tribes of Israel (Matt. 19:28). This rule of the saints will be examined more closely in the next chapter. But the dark side of the millennium appears to be in direct conflict with all the New Testament portrayals of the age to come.

Jesus and the Kingdom

How could there still be tares strewn in the wheat after the day of harvest is over? Did not the Lord teach that the tares, symbolic of the evil men in the world today, are to be totally consumed and separated from the righteous forever? This is what he said:

> Just as the weeds are gathered and burned with fire, so will it be at the close of the age. The Son of man will send his angels, and they will gather out of his kingdom all causes of sin and all evildoers, and throw them into the furnace of fire; there men will weep and gnash their teeth (Matt. 13:40–42).

If Jesus believed that there would be yet another era for sinners to repent and believe the gospel, why did He urge His disciples to "Go out into the highways and hedges, and compel people to come in" (Luke 14:23)? Or why did He repeatedly warn His hearers that if they believe *today* they will be rewarded then, but if they refuse Him today they will be punished then? (Matt. 25:21; John 3:36; 5:24; 6:40).

Christ's positive and descriptive statements about the nature of the future kingdom carry the argument a step further. It will be a "new world," (lit. a re-birth of the world, Matt. 19:28). It will not be some intermediate state, but "the kingdom prepared . . . from the foundation of the world" (Matt. 25:34). For the faithful servant it will be a world where he will "enter into the joy of. . . [his] Master" (Matt. 25:21). Jesus said that the future kingdom is like a great "banquet" where all can expect to share in the bounties and joys of that day (Luke 14:15). Even for the believing thief on the cross next to our Lord, the future was "paradise," first in the heavenly glory with Christ, then in the age to come (Luke 23:43). Clearly, therefore, when the teachings of Jesus are reviewed, the coming kingdom has *no* dark side, no admixture of saints with sinners, and no evil combined with good.

Jesus also would not agree with the premillennarians on the idea that "earthly saints" will somehow mingle with the "heavenly, resurrected saints." This is a crucial point, since apart from "earthly saints" there could never be a generation of "kingdom kids" born with the old sinful nature during the thousand years. In sharp contrast to this train of premillennial thought is Jesus' own teaching on the condition of the saints after His return.

> The sons of this age marry and are given in marriage; but those who are accounted worthy to attain to that age and to the resurrection from the dead neither marry nor are given in marriage, for they cannot die any more, because they are equal to angels and are sons of God, being sons of the resurrection (Luke 20:34–36).

The passage is a contrast between the present age and the age to come. All men who "attain to that age" are to be like the angels; none will father children. So it is appalling to find that the popular view of the age to come still insists on adding "earthly saints" to the kingdom in such a way as to effectively contradict the Lord's plain teaching on the subject!

Paul's Kingdom Teaching

The doctrine of Paul and the apostles on the age to come is no more comfort to the premillennialists than that of Christ in the Gospels. To the Corinthians, Paul wrote: "flesh and blood cannot inherit the kingdom of God" (I Cor. 15:50). However one conceives the resurrected body, it must resemble Jesus' new body; all the perishable parts of "flesh and blood" are eliminated from the kingdom according to this verse. As noted before, the resurrected Christ is already reigning and will reign "until he has put all his enemies under his feet. The last enemy to be destroyed is death" (15:25–26). When this age of warfare comes to an end, then He will in triumph turn all things over to His Father, "that God may be everything to everyone" (15:28). No exegesis of this verse can avoid acknowledging its universal element: all men who share in that future age will belong to the eternal household of God!

Premillennarians attempt to evade this conclusion in I Corinthians by forcing a sudden break between verses 23 and 24, which read as follows: "but each in his own order: Christ the first fruits, then at his coming those who belong to Christ. Then comes the end, when he delivers the kingdom to God the Father after destroying every rule and every authority and power" (I Cor. 15:23-24). A parenthesis to cover the millennium must be inserted here if Paul's teaching is to harmonize with their theory about the age to come. The *then* of "then comes the end" is not actually next in sequence, as the natural flow of Paul's language would normally suggest, but actually a *then* one thousand years later! This expediency is tantamount to wedging in the era of the church between Daniel's sixty-ninth and seventieth week! The obvious mistake in this device is seen in Paul's identification of the day of the resurrection as the day when the "last enemy"—death—is to be destroyed (I Cor. 15:26, 54, 55). This fact by itself is sufficient evidence to deny the millennialists the right to break the sequence of verses 23 and 24. Students of Paul will search in vain for any clue that he considered the age to come to be temporal or intermediary. For Paul, even the natural creation is to be drastically altered on the day of "the redemption of our bodies" (Rom. 8:23). This places his view of the age to come within the language of Revelation 21 and 22, where the total fulfillment of all future blessings comes to pass in the Edenic new world.

Every word by Paul about the coming age is positive. In I Thessalonians it will mean deliverance from wrath (1:10), "glory and joy" in the believers (2:20), being established "in holiness before our God and Father" (3:13), being forever with the Lord (4:17), obtaining salvation and living with him (5:9–10). In his second letter to the Thessalonians he adds, "To this he called you through our Gospel, so that you may obtain the glory of our Lord Jesus Christ" (2:14). To Timothy, the apostle wrote: "Keep ... (yourself) free from reproach until the appearing of our Lord Jesus Christ; and this will be made manifest at the proper time (his appearing) by the blessed and only Sovereign, the King of kings and Lord of lords, who alone has immortality and dwells in unapproachable light, whom no man has ever seen or can see. To him be honor and eternal dominion. Amen" (I Tim. 6:14–16). The appearing of Christ for Paul, therefore, will introduce the eternal kingdom and the final state for all the redeemed in Christ. If there is to be yet another age after this one, but before the final one, Paul is totally silent about it.

Peter's View

Peter's letters give further support to the conclusion that the writers of the New Testament are not premillennialists in the popular use of the term. When facing scoffers who denied the validity of the promise of Christ's coming, the apostle Peter reminded them of the days of Noah when, after a time of grace, the door of the ark was shut and that world destroyed. It is due to the long-suffering of God that the Lord's return seems to be delayed. After all, to Him a wait of a "thousand years" is but one day! Notice that the Lord is concerned that none perish, "but that all come to repentance," (II Peter 3:9, KJV). He means that *this* is the time for repentance and faith; after His coming it will be too late. For God these two thousand years of gospel invitation since Pentecost are merely two days, as if Christ died for us the day before yesterday! Who can set the time for the end and tell how long the patience of God with sinners will last? Yet that day will come! According to Peter, the one event, Christ's second advent, will accomplish both the cleansing of the earth by fire and the establishment of a "new earth in which righteousness dwells" (3:13).

John's Teaching

One more inspired writer of the New Testament deserves to be considered—the apostle John. What he believed to be the nature of the age to come is particularly relevant to the interpretation of Revelation 20. From the Gospel of John we learn that he believed in a general resurrection of the dead. He said, "Do not marvel at this; for the hour is coming when *all* who are in the tombs will hear his voice and come forth, those who have done good, to the resurrection of life, and those who have done evil, to the resurrection of judgment" (John 5:28–29). His statement is comprehensive; all people are in either one or the other category. The "resurrection of life" suggests a new world for the saints in their new bodies, while the "resurrection of judgment" suggests condemnation and separation from God. There is no place in this text for a third group whose fate is yet unresolved at the hour of the resurrection. Evidently John knew nothing about another thousand years for sinners to be saved or to be deceived.

Speaking of the Good Shepherd, John taught that there were "other sheep," not of the Jewish fold, that had to be brought in so that in the final consummation there will be "one flock, one shepherd" (John 10:16). The unity of all the saints of all nations is the intention here, as well as the clear teaching of Jesus throughout His ministry. John uses the phrase "the last day" frequently for the final event of this age. On that day there will take place the resurrection, as Martha declared (John 11:24). Men will be judged by his word on the last day (John 12:48). "In that day you will know that I am in my Father, and you in me, and I in you" (John 14:20). The disciples were assured that when they saw Him again they would rejoice; and "no one will take your joy from you," he said. "In that day you will ask nothing of me" (John 16:22-23). Such knowledge and joy are not to be merely passing experiences but the glorious blessing of eternity in Christ!

John's most beautiful description of the future comes from the fourteenth chapter of his Gospel: "In my Father's house are many rooms;... I go to prepare a place for you." If anyone objects to the application of this passage to the future kingdom, let him read on to discover that Jesus also said, "I will come again and will take you to myself, that where I am you may be also." This is not to deny the presence of the saints with Christ in heaven today, but points out that the "mansions" will be there for all His disciples at his return! The same truth is brought out by John in his first epistle. "We know that when he appears we shall be like him, for we shall see him as he is" (I John 3:2). Thus John sees a great future moment of glory connected with the return of his Lord, which will set the pattern for the age that follows that return. It is a Platonic mind that conceives of *heaven* as somewhere up above the clouds. The biblical view, however, has always pointed to the future climax of this age and the dawning of a new age to fulfill the final promise of redemption. So it is that John was given the vision of the New Jerusalem coming down from heaven to settle once again on this earth. That event will take place only after all wars, judgments, and destinies have been resolved forever.

Summary

This has been an attempt to summarize the teachings of our Lord about the future kingdom and the age to come, as well as the views of Paul, Peter, and John. That the saints will reign at His side in glory and triumph is obvious, but that evildoers will continue to exist in that day is not. In fact, every testimony speaks to the termination of wickedness by the end of this present age. If the last enemy to be destroyed is death, and if that victory is contiguous with the resurrection, and if the resurrection is truly, as Jesus said, "the last day," then no doctrine of an interim state, or future "millennium" with its mixture of good and bad, has any support from the New Testament.

The chart which follows is rightly labeled "The New Testament View of the Ages" because it shows graphically the two advents of the Messiah, the first for redemption and the second for judgment and resurrection. In the Old Testament only one advent had been revealed. The chart also demonstrates the clear distinctions between the three ages, or dispensations, of man: the Edenic world, this present cursed world, and the blessed world to come.

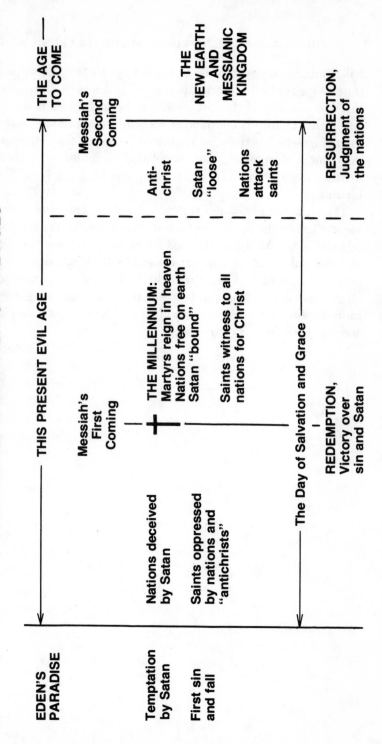

THE NEW TESTAMENT VIEW OF THE AGES

EDEN'S PARADISE

Temptation by Satan

First sin and fall

THIS PRESENT EVIL AGE

Messiah's First Coming

Nations deceived by Satan

Saints oppressed by nations and "antichrists"

The Day of Salvation and Grace

REDEMPTION, Victory over sin and Satan

THE MILLENNIUM:
Martyrs reign in heaven
Nations free on earth
Satan "bound"

Saints witness to all nations for Christ

Anti-christ

Satan "loose"

Nations attack saints

RESURRECTION, Judgment of the nations

THE AGE TO COME

Messiah's Second Coming

THE NEW EARTH AND MESSIANIC KINGDOM

Chapter Five

Where Does
the Millennium
Belong?

Will the events of the thousand years in Revelation 20 happen after Christ's return or before? This is the fundamental question all students of biblical prophecy need to answer. Our comparative studies so far have shown how difficult it is to match the millennial scenes with the rest of the kingdom passages in the Bible, particularly the dark and rebellious ones. Now it is time to look directly at the key passage, Revelation 20:1–10, and its relationship to the surrounding events of the book.

Since there is no break in the narrative between chapters 19 and 20, it would appear at first glance that the events of chapter 20 follow in sequence. First comes the war against the Beast and all bearing his mark, then the binding of Satan, and then the thousand years. However, a number of features will appear to challenge this order. There is good reason to conclude that at this point John broke the sequence to reiterate the great themes of victory for the saints and defeat for the forces of evil. Thus, chapter 20:1–10 may be taken as a return to the present age leading up to the second advent of Christ.

In the pursuit of an answer to this final question, "Where does the millennium belong?" we must not allow ourselves to get bogged down in a debate over a literal versus a nonliteral interpretation. The essential and concrete aspects of the text may not be "spiritualized" out of existence. The martyred and enthroned saints are real, the angel who binds Satan is real, Satan himself is very real, and the wicked nations in revolt against the King are real nations and part of history. The question is not, therefore, which view is the more literal, but which correctly understands the place and purpose of the thousand years.

Of course, the most literal of exegetes will have to confront the extensive use of symbolic language in Revelation, so often borrowed from the apocalyptic passages of the Old Testament. It is obvious that John relished nonliteral terms. What is the basic reality behind such words as "key and chain," "bottomless pit," "dragon and serpent," "prison," "four corners of the earth," and "fire and brimstone"? Could not even the famous "thousand years" be a figure of speech for an extended, but indefinite, period of time?[1]

Those who are convinced that the Lord will come prior to the millennium are properly called "premillennialists." Those who believe that the millennial events will not follow Christ's return are called "amillennialists," but wrongly so. The term itself is an improper mixture of a Greek prefix and the Latin term for "one thousand." Furthermore, it is both unfair and inaccurate to ascribe a label meaning "no millennium" to a view that believes that a very real millennium is in progress right now. A "present-day millennium," stretching from our Lord's first coming to His second, can be just as literal as a millennium which hasn't started yet. Since the New Testament writers frequently refer to this final phase of the world

---

1. J. Barton Payne, *Encyclopedia of Biblical Prophecy* (New York: Harper and Row, 1973), p. 626. Payne says that a kingdom of "limited extent" is the meaning of the number 1,000.

as "the latter days," it would be correct to call this point of view *historical millennialism*, or a "millennium of the last days." There are various approaches to the Book of Revelation within the group of interpreters called *amillennialists*, but the one here represented views the eschatological events, both of Jesus' teachings and of John's, as running the entire length of the centuries from the time of Christ to the last day of this age. This requires that the "thousand years" be taken figuratively for a long, albeit limited, period.

There are three scenes running concurrently through the thousand years of Revelation 20:1–10. Each one needs to be examined carefully if we are to arrive at a contextual answer to the question of where the millennium belongs. These three may be summarized as follows:

A. Satan Bound. Satan, who had been deceiving the nations, is bound and prevented from doing so for a thousand years; then he is set free to deceive them again (20:2–3).

B. Martyred Saints Reign. The souls of the beheaded and faithful saints are seen on thrones, alive and reigning with Christ for a thousand years (20:4–6).

C. Nations in Revolt. The nations which had been previously deceived by Satan are set free from his power for a thousand years, then led once more by Satan into a battle against the saints and their city (20:7–10).

Satan Bound

It is not difficult to understand why someone might conclude that the "binding of Satan" belongs to some future age rather than to this one. The devil's operations in our world today are too obvious to deny. Furthermore, the New Testament refers to this age as an evil one and to Satan as the "ruler of this world" (John 12:31). For Paul, he is "the prince of the power of the air, the spirit that is now at work in the sons of disobedience" (Eph. 2:2). Believers are warned to resist his power and to put on their armor against his "wiles" (6:11).

The argument is not closed at this point, however, for there is another example in the New Testament which shows Satan to have been defeated at the cross and his power greatly curtailed. When Jesus drove out the demons He was actually proclaiming His authority over Satan and the arrival of His kingdom. He said, "How can one enter a strong man's house-... unless he first binds the strong man?" (Matt. 12:29). As the disciples also found success in casting out demons, the Lord exclaimed: "I saw Satan fall like lightning from heaven" (Luke 10:18). This was a metaphoric way of saying that the devil's power had been overcome by the King's envoys. We know that Satan was cast down when Christ was lifted up (John 12:31); thus it was Calvary's victory that broke the grip of the devil on men and nations. The Gospels clearly teach that the devil's control and power over the peoples of the world has been weakened since the first advent of Christ, (cf. Heb. 2:14).

There is an explicit declaration of the restraint placed upon the evil forces of this age in Paul's second letter to the Thessalonians. Although lawlessness is working in the world, the full force of wickedness is not allowed because "he who now restrains it will do so until he is out of the way" (II Thess. 2:7). It is reasonable to believe that it is the divine power of the Holy Spirit at work in the hearts of all men which effectively limits their potential to do wrong. Furthermore, the form of the evil here is identical to that in Revelation. The moment the restraint is off, the Antichrist appears! Paul's description of the "man of lawlessness" closely matches John's description of the Beast. Both are deceivers; both pretend to be a god and demand worship; both work wonders and miracles; both lead the masses of humanity into bloodshed and revolt against the Lord; both are destroyed by the coming of Christ in judgment (cf. II Thess. 2 with Rev. 13, 17, 19).

John makes it very clear in his final book that Satan's area of power is closely guarded and controlled by God. Only after an angel with a key opens the "bottomless pit" can the demons come out (9:2–6). The Beast has to be brought up from the pit at God's command (11:7–8). He is later allowed to make war on the saints (13:7). All of this language supports the secondary line of thought in the New Testament, which states that in some very real sense the devil is "bound" and no longer free to deceive the nations as he did before Christ.

A graphic analysis of this alteration in Satan's role is supplied in the diagram below.

Old Testament Period	Pentecostal Period	Endtime Period
SATAN LOOSE	**SATAN BOUND**	**SATAN LOOSE**
Nations deceived by satanic rulers	Nations no longer deceived by a satanic ruler.	Nations again deceived by Satan and the Antichrist.
People of God oppressed	Nations of world reached by gospel	Saints attacked

Precise boundaries are impossible in a chart such as this, nor are they essential to follow the gist of John's argument. Knowing the prophecies of Ezekiel and Daniel so well, John would have had in mind the "beasts" and the "little horns" of Daniel's super–nations (who were guilty of terrible persecutions and abominations) when he referred to the deception of the nations by the devil (Rev. 20:3). He also lived through the horror of the Roman emperors who demanded to be worshiped as gods and who tortured the Christians for their faith.

From the apostle's perspective, therefore, the binding of Satan was a message of encouragement to the churches. The day was coming when the devil could no longer take control of the world powers through some wicked king or tyrant. John may have recalled the Master's words of hope given at Caesarea Philippi: "I will build my church; and the gates of hell shall not prevail against it" (Matt. 16:18, KJV). John also heard the marching orders of the church to "Go therefore and make disciples of all nations" (Matt. 28:19). The explosion of spiritual power at Pentecost would lead the Christians to "the end of the earth" (Acts 1:8). All of this world activity would become feasible with the binding of Satan.

But when the long period of freedom from Satan's control ends, once again the devil will be set loose on the world for a very brief time. Could this unleashing of Satan take place *twice* in the distant future? Would it happen at the close of this world, and then happen all over again at the close of the messianic kingdom? There is evidence against this double view. A voice from heaven told John that the devil "knows that his time is short" (Rev. 12:12). This apprehension within the events scheduled for the end of this age strongly suggests that Satan will attack the saints for the *last* time when this world terminates. At the final battle scene his false prophet and beast will be destroyed and all evil men with them. It is reasonable, therefore, to take the "little while" of the millennial passage (20:3) as the "short time" of chapter 12.

The New Testament teaches, in fulfillment of Psalm 110, that Christ is now reigning and will reign until all of His enemies are destroyed, "and the last enemy to be destroyed is death" (I Cor. 15:26). The devil, as the principal of Christ's enemies, will therefore be forever put away at the consummation of this world and before the glorious kingdom gets underway (cf. Matt. 28:18 and Eph. 6:12, 13).

The Reigning Saints

In order to identify the saints and martyrs John saw on the thrones of this second millennial scene we need to agree on two basic concepts. First, the apostle John had a message with direct application to the suffering Christians of his own day; and second, the throne scene here is linked directly to the other throne scenes in the Book of Revelation.

Our first assumption raises again the issue of the "preterist" versus the "futurist" view of the Apocalypse. One view holds that John saw only the immediate affairs of his lifetime under Rome; the other says he saw only the events of the far distant future at the return of Christ. When put this way, however, the issue is poorly defined. We know for a certainty that John was waiting for the return of the Lord in his own lifetime. This is indicated by such remarks as "the time is near" (1:3), "what must soon take place" (22:6), "Surely I am coming soon" (22:20). He could not say these things, knowing that the Messiah's return would bring the age to a close, without assuming that the persecutions around him were the final ones, at least potentially. John gives the evil powers a short period to struggle and the saints a thousand years to enjoy their reward. This is the "preterist" point of view.

"Futurists" tend to overlook these first-century fulfillments in their demand for detailed predictions of the very last days. What is needed is a view which spans the intervening time and blends the tribulations of John's day with the final ones. The tension between John's expectation of the Messiah's nearness and his vision of the millennium is a major problem for the amillennarians, but the viewpoint represented by Augustine and held by myself is both "preteret" and "futurist"; the Book of Revelations prophesies the entire age and its end events.

Jesus' eschatological teachings also moved easily from the first century to the last days. With warnings to His disciples of the "antichrists" they would encounter and of the terrible destruction of Jerusalem about to take place, He prepared them for the ministry they would have in their lifetime. Their generation would "not pass away till all these things take place," He said (Matt. 24:34). But at the same time He jumped to the very last day of the age when He said: "Two men will be in the field; one is taken and one is left" (24:40). As in the days of Noah, the one "taken" will be swept away into judgment, and the one "left" will enter the glorious kingdom. Our Lord deliberately hid from His disciples the extension of the days of Pentecost for these two thousand years, so that every generation of believers may heed His admonition, "Be ready; for the Son of Man is coming at an hour you do not expect" (24:44).

John should not be faulted for doing exactly what our Lord did in this regard by moving abruptly from his own times to the final events, but always giving the churches reason to believe the Lord's return was at hand. Both "preterists" and "futurists" have a part of the truth. Much of what John saw and wrote was related to the Roman powers and the experiences of the first-century Christians. It was for their comfort that John was given a series of visions of the heavenly throneroom. All who die in Christ are "alive and well" in the presence of the Lamb of God. John observed them as conquering ones seated with Christ on his throne (Rev. 3:21), or again, as the "souls of those who had been slain for the word of God" under the altar (6:9). Their number is "one hundred and forty-four thousand," all of them redeemed from the earth and singing before Christ's heavenly throne (14:3). So obvious are these parallels to the throne-scene in chapter 20 that any denial of this fact will mean ignoring the larger context completely.

The early church called them "martyrs" and "confessors." Are we to take these titles in the narrow sense, leaving out the other believers who have died peacefully in their beds and gone to glory? Ladd argues for a more general interpretation. "The language suggests two different groups: one group to whom judgment was given, and a smaller group who are martyrs of the great tribulation."[2] One could even argue for three groups in the text: the judging group, the martyred group, and the faithful group who refused to worship the Beast. The problem with Ladd's view is that he takes the "great tribulation" to mean only the far off and final one, which would hold no comfort for the believers facing death in John's day. This does not sound like the natural meaning John's readers would have ascribed to these words. Every period of martyrdom should be included, but how can we eliminate the "preterist" side of the question entirely? Our modern perspective is actually a disadvantage in arriving at the author's message in this passage. Every saint is honored after death and assured a place in heaven's throneroom!

Premillennialists, however, have gone far beyond the literal sense of the text in their identification of these reigning saints. They see both heavenly and earthly saints forming a new "Israel" under a new Davidic king in fulfillment of all the political promises of the Old Testament. They believe that resurrected saints will mingle with unresurrected saints in that future kingdom, a view which the passage plainly denies. Whatever one makes of the phrase "first resurrection" in Revelation 20:6, it has to be inclusive of all who reign with Christ. If, therefore, it is understood to be the physical resurrection of believers, then it may not include the tribulation survivors who are yet unresurrected. Remember that for the premillennarians it is essential that babies be born with sinful hearts as a means of repopulating the earth. It is from these sons of the saints that the "kingdom kids" appear, and from them are comprised the evil nations within the kingdom. Nothing in this passage or any other remotely suggests this idea for the future reign of the Messiah.

---

2. George Ladd, A Commentary on the Revelation of John (Grand Rapids: W. B. Eerdmans, 1972), p. 263.

The search for the true meaning of the "first resurrection" in the text is not an easy one. The premillennarian interpretation has already been referred to: all believers will be raised only at the coming of Christ, with the "rest of the dead" remaining in their graves until the thousand years are over. Amillennialists differ widely in their views of this subject. Augustine held to the believer's regeneration as the "first resurrection."[3] B. B. Warfield concluded that it meant the glorification of the believers and the intermediate state following death.[4] For Albertus Pieters it is only a symbol of the triumph for which the martyrs gave their lives.[5] In the opinion of this writer, Warfield's view comes closest to John's intention.

We are not forced to conclude that if the second resurrection (a term never mentioned in the text) is physical, then the "first resurrection" must also be physical. In spite of Dean Alford's famous words about the two resurrections,[6] the "aliveness" of the saints is the point of the scene. The Christian passes "from death unto life" when he believes, according to John 5:24, and the new life in Christ is frequently called a "resurrection" (Rom. 6:11; Eph. 2:4, 5; Col. 3:1). But here John observed glorified saints who had died yet had remained alive and able to sing the praises of the Lamb. Revelation 20 was given to the churches to comfort them in respect to loved ones who had died and gone to be with

---

3. For a summary of Augustine's millennial views see O. T. Allis, *Prophecy and the Church* (Philadelphia: Presbyterian and Reformed Publishing Company, 1945), pp. 2–5.

4. B. B. Warfield, "The Millennium and the Apocalypse," *Biblical Doctrines* (New York: Oxford University Press, 1929), p. 653.

5. Albertus Pieters, *Studies in the Revelation of St. John* (Grand Rapids: W. B. Eerdmans, 1954), p. 304.

6. Henry Alford, *The Greek Testament* (Boston: Lee and Shepard, 1872), vol. IV, p. 732. Alford's statement on the two resurrections is as follows: "If in such a passage the first resurrection may be understood to mean *spiritual* rising with Christ, while the second means *literal* rising from the grave, then there is an end of all significance in language."

Christ. As in the earlier scenes of the heavenly throneroom, here again the believers are enjoying their reward. The vision portrays them in white robes as if they had already been resurrected, yet they belong to the intermediate state and await the consummation and the resurrection day just as we on earth.

Nations in Revolt

A study of the "nations" as described in the New Testament will demonstrate that they usually were thought of as godless Gentiles and unbelievers. It was the duty of the churches to win them to the faith, but it was the doctrine of the church that they were lost in sin and living under the domain of Satan. Gog and Magog had become a symbol among the first-century Jews and Christians for the pagan hordes existing around the fringes of the civilized world. Time and again they had invaded the land of Palestine with devastating effects. Daniel saw them as beasts that would come and make war on the saints (Dan. 7:21). Ezekiel foretold the coming of Gog and his armies to invade the land. Zechariah knew that the Holy City would be captured and devastated. All this had literally come to pass, and it witnesses to the sequence of Daniel's four kingdoms: Babylon, Persia, Greece, and Rome. Now John foresees that the nations will be released from Satan's power for a long time, only to fall under it once more at the end of the world when they rebel against the Messiah.

There is an unmistakable continuity of nations in the millennial passages. The same nations are deceived by the devil, then not deceived for a thousand years, then deceived again. Why not consider these events as actual and historical, placing them within the world of sinful peoples of our present age? The scene is an earthly one, in sharp contrast with the heavenly throneroom, where the saints are seen "reigning with Christ." What happens to them during the thousand years, John does not mention, but his implication is clear: they will enjoy a long day of relative freedom from the domination of satanically-inspired rulers and oppressive governments. Correlating this fact to these intervening years since Pentecost is not a simple task. The world has always had areas of cruel domination by evil kings and leaders. Generally speaking, however, the freedom for men to believe and receive the gospel has been worldwide. We have witnessed the victories of the Holy Spirit and the growing church of Christ which, like the mustard tree, continues to grow.

Much in the Bible indicates a dark future for the unconverted nations of the earth. Evil days are ahead, said the apostles; the "man of sin" must be revealed, and the people will follow him to their own final destruction. It is not out of place, therefore, for John to see the final short period of this world as a time of war and bloodshed—particularly as a time when the battle lines will be drawn between the city of God and those who gather to attack it. This final millennial scene fits best into the concluding events of the present day and age, which has been established by God as the time for human freedom to run its course and conflicts to occur. All of the peoples of the world are blessed in the meantime by the "good news" of God's grace and salvation.

Final Resurrection and Judgment

If the three scenes of the millennium rightly belong to this age, then the resurrection and judgment ought to follow immediately thereafter; and so they do. No mention of physical resurrection occurs in John's book previous to this second part of chapter 20 about the great white throne. In order to gather all men of all ages and nations before His throne, God commanded that the graves be opened. "And the sea gave up the dead in it. Death and Hades gave up the dead in them, and were all judged by what they had done" (Rev. 20:13). All whose names were not in the Book of Life were thrown into the lake of fire; "This is the second death!" (20:14). To die twice suggests that sinners receive their bodies a second time for the purpose of standing on trial before God, and perhaps also as a reminder of what they are about to lose forever. Death is the separation of soul and body; therefore, the great white throne scene begins with the physical and general resurrection of all the peoples of the earth.

Can we trust John to teach the same doctrine in all of his writings? If so, then the general resurrection at the end of this world was his basic view and needs to be kept in mind at all times when reading through his Book of Revelation. In his gospel he quoted the Master, using the most unequivocal language possible: "the hour is coming when *all* who are in the tombs will hear his voice and come forth, those who have done good, to the resurrection of life, and those who have done evil, to the resurrection of judgment" (John 5:28–29). In the Revelation, John places this hour of resurrection at the very end of all other events and just prior to the dawning of the final state.

Premillennialists often speak of seven judgments, but the Scriptures speak of only one final judgment for the nations. Believers are told that they will "not come into judgment," yet will be tested for their faithfulness and for their works built on the foundation of Christ (I Cor. 3:13; Rom. 14:10–12; II Tim. 4:8). Furthermore, according to the instruction of Jesus, the "sheep and the goats" will stand before Him at the same time. When He "comes in his glory, and all the angels with him" (Matt. 25:31), He will then judge the nations and settle the destiny of everyone. A most unfortunate error has evolved from this passage in Matthew 25. It is the mistaken idea that groups of people will be judged as one nation, according to the way they treated the Jews. Careful exegesis of

the passage will refute this view.[7] In the Greek text of this
passage the forms change to masculine plurals and refer to the
people themselves, not the nations as a whole. The basis of
judgment has to do with the way individuals received the
gospel of Christ and "His brethren"; that is, the envoys of the
gospel whom Christ sent out to all nations.

The timing of the final judgment, therefore, is the end of
this age, the day of the "harvest" which Malachi saw clearly.
"For behold, the day comes, burning like an oven, when all
the arrogant and all evildoers will be stubble; the day that
comes shall burn them up, says the Lord of hosts. . . . But for
you who fear my name the sun of righteousness shall rise,
shall rise, with healing in its wings" (Mal. 4:1-2).

The Final State

Where does the millennium belong in relation to the final
state of the saints described in Revelation 21 and 22? Some
aspects of the thousand-year reign bear a close likeness to the
new earth, but others are so contrary as to make the identification impossible. The millennial age is temporal, and its
termination point is clearly marked by the revolt of Gog and
Magog. But the final state is endless and secure from all forms
of evil. During the millennium the saints join the Messiah in
his heavenly realm, but in the final state the Messiah joins the
saints in the New Jerusalem on earth. The people of the millennium are a mixed lot—saints and sinners, believers and
unbelievers. The people of the final state will all be wholly
sanctified and have their names written in the Book of Life
(Rev. 21:27).

---

7. Alen H. McNeile, *The Gospel According to St. Matthew* (London:
MacMillan and Co., 1915), p. 369. McNeile points out that the Greek term
for *those* (25:34) refers to the individuals which comprise the "nations."

There is no mention of an earthly paradise in the language of Revelation 20, or even a suggestion that the earth will become a kind of Garden of Eden during the millennial age. But the final state will most assuredly be a perfect environment on a universal scale. This is clear in that the imagery of Genesis 2 is used again by John to picture the transformed earth in Revelation 22. It is also supported by the use of quotations and allusions taken from Isaiah's utopian kingdom passages (Isa. 11:6–10; 65:17–25) and employed to describe the eternal dwelling place of the saints (Rev. 21).

The "marriage supper of the Lamb" will not take place during the course of the thousand years, nor will it occur during the final battles against the Beast and all who wear his mark. It will happen at the inauguration of the eternal state (Rev. 21:2). Only after the destinies of all men have been resolved and the new heavens and the new earth have been created will the great moment for the wedding arrive. John sees the New Jerusalem "coming down out of heaven from God, prepared as a bride adorned for her husband" (Rev. 21:2). This sight is followed by the Lord's words which are taken from the ancient marriage covenant: "And he will live with them, and they will be his people." No one should overlook these features that mark this passage as the marriage ceremony between God and His holy ones, His elect of all ages, "the Bride, the wife of the Lamb" (Rev. 21:9).

It should be remembered that the bride had "made herself ready" back at the time of the conflict between the armies of heaven and those of the beast (Rev. 19:7–16). This signifies that as the final moments of the age transpire, the body of the saved ones who comprise the bride becomes complete. All who are to be redeemed by the blood of the Lamb will be included. Furthermore, it is clear that the wedding time has come, the guests are invited, and the feast is announced (Rev. 19:7–9). Some interpreters conclude that the marriage feast must take place during the final battles of the Christ and the

Antichrist, or at least before the end of this age. This is due to the fact that they assume that the thousand years will follow the Lord's coming in Revelation 19, and such a delay of the marriage does not fit the context. If the millennial age, however, is a recapitulation of this present period between the first and second advents, then the problem vanishes. The wedding announced at the close of this age (Rev. 19) will take place a short time later at the dawning of the age to come (Rev. 21).

It has been shown throughout this discussion that the Scriptures view human history as moving toward the judgment of this world and the establishment of the world to come. The only state that fits the kingdom prophecies is the final one in the last two chapters of the Bible. The millennial age in no way can lay claim to this support. In spite of this fact, it is a common practice for Bible teachers to consider the messianic-age passages as part of the thousand years of Revelation 20:1–10 and leave little or nothing for the final state. Many interpreters apparently forget that in the final state the saints are returned to this earth, and the eternal kingdom they share with the Messiah is an earthly one. This is the kingdom of which the prophets spoke: "Of the increase of his government and of peace there will be no end" (Isa. 9:7).

Summary

From the one and only explicit millennial passage in the Bible three concurrent scenes emerge: the one of Satan bound, the one of the reigning saints, and the one of the nations in revolt. Only one of these is present on earth in the literal sense of the term—the nations in revolt. The binding of Satan according to all other New Testament evidence is a restriction of his movements relative to his control over the nations through some antichrist figure. The saints are in the heavenly throneroom, rewarded for their faithfulness until death, and rejoicing in the anticipation of the final victories by the Lamb over His enemies.

All of these scenes fit the present conditions of the earth below and the glorified saints above. The messianic kingdom is still to come, and when it does come it will be on earth in fulfillment of the Old Testament prophecies as well as in fulfillment of the words of Jesus and the apostles. But it will not be temporal or limited, or marred by future wars or revolts. The bride will return to the earth to be joined forever with the Bridegroom; the nations will have been judged and the wicked cast into hell, some for the second time; and the new earth will become the paradise of the servants of God for ever and ever (Rev. 22:1–5).

The biblical millennium, therefore, is not the glorious age to come, but this present era for giving the message of salvation to the nations. "And this gospel of the kingdom will be preached throughout the whole world, as a testimony to all nations; and then the end will come" (Matt. 24:14).